YOUR PASSPORT TO
SOUTH AFRICA

by Dr. Artika R. Tyner

CAPSTONE PRESS
a capstone imprint

Published by Capstone Press, an imprint of Capstone
1710 Roe Crest Drive, North Mankato, Minnesota 56003
capstonepub.com

Library of Congress Cataloging-in-Publication Data
Names: Tyner, Artika R., author.
Title: Your passport to South Africa / by Artika R. Tyner.
Other titles: World passport.
Description: North Mankato, MN : Capstone Press, an imprint of Capstone, [2023] | Series: World passport | Includes bibliographical references and index. | Audience: Ages 8-11 | Audience: Grades 4-6 | Summary: "What is it like to live in or visit South Africa? What makes South Africa's culture unique? Explore the geography, traditions, and daily lives of South Africans"— Provided by publisher.
Identifiers: LCCN 2022028954 (print) | LCCN 2022028955 (ebook) | ISBN 9781666390247 (hardcover) | ISBN 9781666390193 (paperback) | ISBN 9781666390209 (pdf) | ISBN 9781666390223 (kindle edition) Subjects: LCSH: South Africa—Juvenile literature.
Classification: LCC DT1719 .T96 2023 (print) | LCC DT1719 (ebook) | DDC 968—dc23/eng/20220617
LC record available at https://lccn.loc.gov/2022028954
LC ebook record available at https://lccn.loc.gov/2022028955

Editorial Credits
Editor: Carrie Sheely; Designer: Elyse White; Media Researcher: Morgan Walters; Production Specialist: Tori Abraham

Image Credits
Alamy: davidwallphoto.com, 19, Iconpix, 11, imageBROKER, 8, REUTERS, 9; Associated Press: Denis Farrell, 18; Capstone Press: Eric Gohl, 5; Getty Images: Foto24, 25, Gallo Images, 21, GUILLEM SARTORIO, 27, Popperfoto, 1, Sam Barnes, 29, Yevhenii Dubinko, (stamps) design element; Shutterstock: Alessia Pierdomenico, 12, Damian Ryszawy, 17, InnaFelker, 23, Flipser, (passport pages) design element, meunierd, 6, michaeljung, (bottom) cover, MicroOne, (stamps) design element, pingebat, (stamps) design element, Save nature and wildlife, (map) cover, WitR, 16

CONTENTS

Words in **bold** are in the glossary.

CHAPTER ONE

WELCOME TO SOUTH AFRICA!

The sun shines bright on a Saturday morning. South Africans gather in a marketplace to buy food for the upcoming week. There are fresh fruits and vegetables on display in baskets. They include tomatoes, apricots, coconuts, and bananas. Seafood is ready for people to buy too.

People talk happily to one another, and the space is filled with joy and laughter. Some people say hello to their friends in Zulu: *Sawubona*. Others greet each other by saying "Molo." It is from the Xhosa language.

MAP OF SOUTH AFRICA

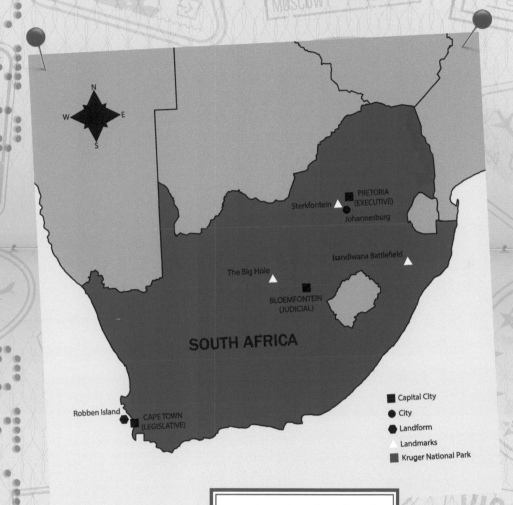

Sterkfontein

PRETORIA
(EXECUTIVE)

Johannesburg

Isandlwana Battlefield

The Big Hole

BLOEMFONTEIN
(JUDICIAL)

SOUTH AFRICA

Robben Island

CAPE TOWN
(LEGISLATIVE)

■ Capital City
● City
⬡ Landform
△ Landmarks
■ Kruger National Park

Explore South Africa's
cities and landmarks.

People wear traditional Zulu clothing at a presentation in Cape Town.

South Africa is known as the "Rainbow Nation." This is because of the rich **diversity** of South Africa. There is diversity in the people, **cultures**, languages, and land. More than 60 million people live in South Africa. Eleven official languages are spoken there. Some South Africans can speak more than two languages.

Many **ethnic** groups live in South Africa. The largest group is the Zulus. They mostly live in the KwaZulu-Natal Province and Gauteng Province. The second largest group is the Xhosa. They live mainly in the Eastern Cape and Western Cape provinces.

FACT FILE

OFFICIAL NAME: ....REPUBLIC OF SOUTH AFRICA
POPULATION: 60,970,000
LAND AREA: ....471,445 SQ. MI. (1,221,037 SQ KM)
CAPITALS: ....PRETORIA (EXECUTIVE),
                                                          BLOEMFONTEIN (JUDICIAL),
                                                          CAPE TOWN (LEGISLATIVE)
MONEY: ....SOUTH AFRICAN RAND
GOVERNMENT:.........................CONSTITUTIONAL DEMOCRACY
LANGUAGE: ....THERE ARE ELEVEN OFFICIAL LANGUAGES
IN SOUTH AFRICA. THEY ARE AFRIKAANS, ENGLISH, NDEBELE, PEDI,
SOTHO, SWATI, TSONGA, TSWANA, VENDA, XHOSA, AND ZULU.

GEOGRAPHY: South Africa is located in the southern part of
the continent of Africa. It borders the countries of Namibia,
Botswana, Mozambique, Zimbabwe, and Eswatini. The small
country of Lesotho is completely bordered by South African
land. The Atlantic Ocean is to the west of South Africa and
the Indian Ocean is to the east.

NATURAL RESOURCES: South Africa has diamonds, gold,
iron ore, platinum, manganese, chromium, copper, uranium,
 silver, beryllium, and titanium.

CHAPTER TWO

HISTORY OF SOUTH AFRICA

South Africa has a long history. More than 20,000 years ago, people called the San or Bushmen settled in South Africa. The San are related to the Khoekhoe. Both groups are the country's early **Indigenous** people.

Visitors can see rock drawings from the San on the Sevilla Rock Art Trail in South Africa.

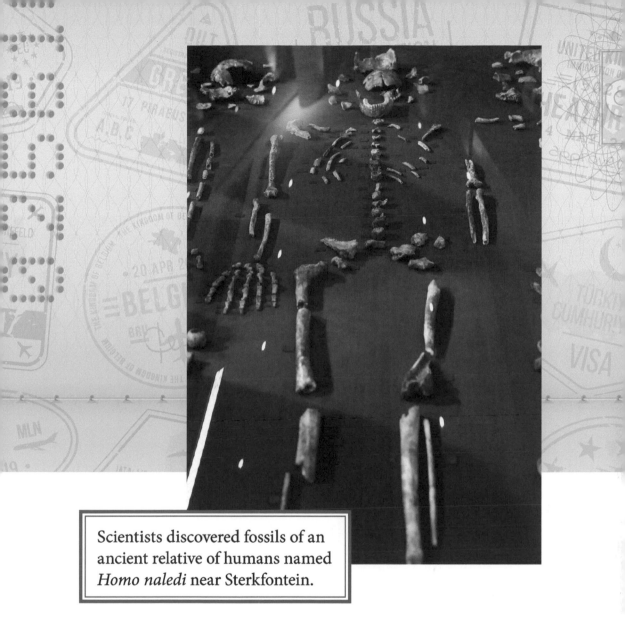

Scientists discovered fossils of an ancient relative of humans named *Homo naledi* near Sterkfontein.

South Africa is known as the "Cradle of Humankind." Many people visit a place in northern South Africa called Sterkfontein. Scientists discovered some of the earliest human **fossils** there. Some of the fossils are 2 million years old.

European countries took the land of the Indigenous people through violence and force. In the 1400s, European ships stopped on the shores of South Africa for supplies. In 1652, the Netherlands founded the city of Cape Town. Dutch farmers called the Boers began settling there. In 1806, wars between European nations left Great Britain in control of the Cape Town **colony**.

THE FIGHT FOR FREEDOM

Some people did not want to be controlled by Great Britain. They fought for freedom. In 1879, fighting broke out between the British and Zulus. On January 22, King Cetshwayo of the Zulu nation led more than 20,000 warriors to fight against the British. They defeated the British in this battle. Today, there is a monument in honor of these warriors at Isandlwana Battlefield.

As fighting continued, the British had more weapons and resources. They defeated the Zulus and took the land.

The Zulu Memorial at Isandlwana Battlefield was built to look like a necklace that Zulu warriors made and wore.

In 1910, under British control, four colonies were declared one nation now known as South Africa. For nearly 50 years, South Africa was ruled by an all-white government. Black people were assigned to certain "homelands" based on their ethnicity. Black people were a majority but owned only 13 percent of the land. Whites were 1/7 of the population but had 87 percent of the land. Black people were treated as second-class citizens on their land.

SOUTH AFRICA'S FREEDOM FIGHTERS

Nelson Mandela

A young lawyer, Nelson Mandela, fought against the practice of racial **segregation** known as **apartheid**. He was the president of a political party called the African National Congress (ANC). The ANC was banned by the government from 1960 to 1990. In 1962, Mandela was arrested for his acts against the government. After a trial, he was put in prison.

TIMELINE OF SOUTH AFRICAN HISTORY

ABOUT 2000 BCE–1500 CE:
The Bantu move across the continent of Africa, eventually reaching South Africa.

1500 CE: The San and Khoekhoe communities are in eastern and western South Africa.

1488: Portuguese explorer Bartolomeu Dias is the first European settler to arrive in South Africa. He names the area where he arrived Cape of Good Hope.

1650s: Whites enslave people from Africa, the East Indies, and Southeast Asia to work on farms.

1651: The Dutch send Jan van Riebeeck to South Africa to set up the Dutch East India Company.

1910: Four colonies come together to form the Union of South Africa.

1948: The policy of apartheid is adopted by the National Party.

1950: South Africans are classified into racial categories. The Group Areas Act is also passed. It divides areas into segregated sections.

1991: South Africa repeals apartheid laws.

1994: The first national election is open to everyone. Nelson Mandela is elected president of South Africa.

On June 16, 1976, Black students organized a protest now called the Soweto Uprising. The youth were fighting against a requirement that students be taught Afrikaans. This was the language of the European colonizers. More than 600 people were killed, and thousands were injured. June 16 is now recognized as a national holiday, Youth Day. It honors the courage of Black youth as they fought for freedom.

In 1990, after serving 27 years in prison, Nelson Mandela was freed by President F.W. de Klerk. He continued his work to end apartheid. In 1994, South Africa had its first **democratic** election. It was the first time that South Africans of all skin colors and backgrounds were allowed to vote. On May 10, 1994, Nelson Mandela became the first Black president of South Africa. A new government formed.

RUSSIA
IMMIGRATION

OUT

GREECE

UNITED KI
IMMIGRATION
(5028

Young protesters surround a burning bus during the Soweto Uprising.

JOHANNESBURG

People formed Johannesburg in 1886 when gold was discovered in the area. Today, more than 5 million people live in this bustling city. The history of apartheid shaped the city's neighborhoods by leaving Black South Africans in slums. One example is Soweto, which was an area for Black people.

CHAPTER THREE

EXPLORE SOUTH AFRICA

South Africa is only one percent of the Earth's surface. But it is home to a wide variety of wildlife and plants. South Africa has nearly 10 percent of the world's bird, fish, and plant **species**. South Africa has around six percent of the world's mammal and reptile species.

Tourists go on safaris to see the animals in their natural living areas. They come to see elephants, buffalo, lions, leopards, and rhinoceroses. Many people enjoy going on safaris at Kruger National Park.

People on safari in Kruger National Park wait as rhinoceroses cross the road.

The Big Hole closed to mining in 1914.
Today, it's a popular tourist attraction.

South Africa has several natural and manmade
landmarks. The Big Hole in Kimberley is an open pit
and underground mine. In 1871, many people came
to look for diamonds at Kimberley. They dug for
these precious gems. The Big Hole is one of the largest
hand-dug pits in the world.

FACT

The Cape horseshoe bat is a kind of bat found
only in southern parts of Africa. The bat's name
comes from its horseshoe-shaped nose parts.

South Africa also has many historical sites. In Mamelodi, a statue honors Solomon Mahlangu. The Steve Biko statue is located in East London. Mahlangu and Biko were freedom fighters who worked toward racial justice.

The bronze statue of Solomon Mahlangu was first shown to the public in 2005.

The Constitutional Court is the highest court. It is located on Constitutional Hill in Johannesburg. The hill was once a fort where prisoners were held.

ROBBEN ISLAND

Robben Island is located in Table Bay. It once had a jail to hold political prisoners. Nelson Mandela was imprisoned there. The old prison is now a museum that people can visit.

Tourists visit Robben Island Prison.

CHAPTER FOUR
DAILY LIFE

Families are an important part of daily life. Many people live together in extended families with grandparents, aunts, uncles, cousins, and other relatives. This has shaped the sense of community in the country. The word *ubuntu* is used in South Africa. This is a reminder that our humanity unites us as one.

South African foods reflect many cultures. Family, friends, and neighbors gather to enjoy meals. On the weekends, they may host barbecues or catch fresh fish at Kalk Bay.

Each meal is filled with delicious flavors and fresh ingredients. Popular foods include *mielie*, or corn, and *boerewors*, a kind of sausage. Mealie pap is a traditional porridge.

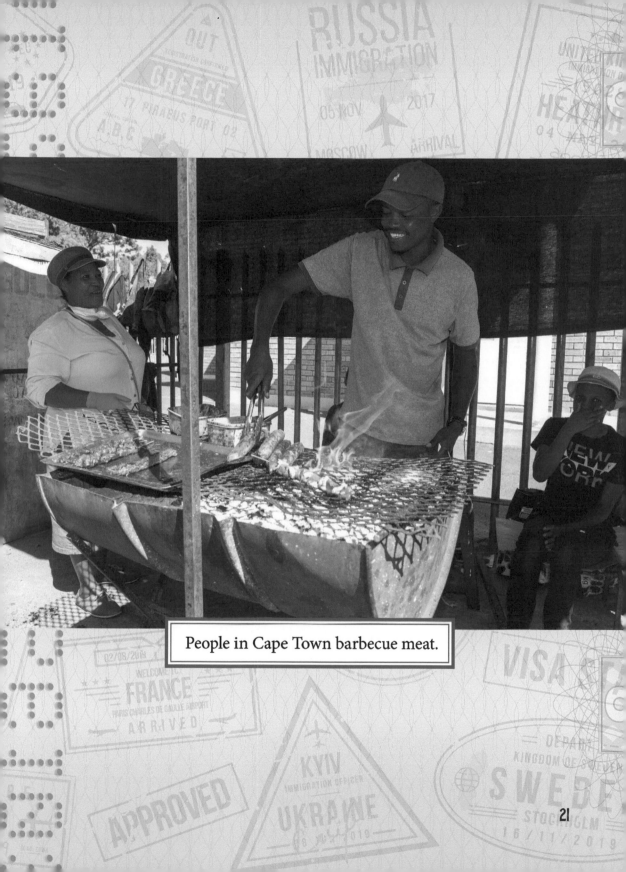

People in Cape Town barbecue meat.

BROWN PUDDING

South African Brown Pudding is a dessert. It is the perfect finishing touch after eating a delicious dinner. With the help of an adult, you can make brown pudding at home.

Cake Ingredients:
- 2 cups white sugar
- 4 eggs
- 2 teaspoons baking soda
- ½ teaspoon salt
- 2 cups flour
- 2 teaspoons baking powder
- 2 ½ tablespoons apricot jam
- 2 cups milk
- 3 tablespoons distilled white vinegar

Sauce Ingredients:
- 1 ½ cups sugar
- 1 cup water
- 1 cup milk
- 2 teaspoons vanilla
- powdered sugar

Brown Pudding Directions:
1. Preheat oven to 350ºF.
2. Mix sugar and eggs with a spoon in a large bowl until light and fluffy. Stir in the flour, baking powder, baking soda, salt, vinegar, and apricot jam. Pour in milk and stir until well combined. Spoon the batter into a greased baking dish.
3. Bake in oven for 60 to 70 minutes, or until a knife inserted into the center comes out clean. Poke the baked pudding several times with a fork.
4. To make the sauce, put sugar, water, milk, butter, and vanilla in a saucepan and stir over medium heat. When the mixture comes to a boil, remove it from heat and slowly pour the sauce over the hot pudding.
5. Sprinkle powdered sugar on top. Serve warm.

ARTS AND MUSIC

Families enjoy music and concerts. Famous choirs are the Zulu choir Ladysmith Black Mambazo and the Soweto Gospel Choir. The songs of Miriam Makeba, known as "Mama Africa," are recognized around the world.

Families also celebrate arts and culture. The National Arts Festival is a yearly event. People gather for 11 days in the city of Makhanda. It is the largest art event on the continent.

A jazz band performs in Cape Town.

CHAPTER FIVE

HOLIDAYS AND CELEBRATIONS

Many holidays honor South Africa's history. Heritage Day is celebrated on September 24. It recognizes the many languages, arts, foods, and music of South Africa.

Human Rights Day is March 21. It is dedicated to those who lost their lives in the township of Sharpeville while protesting against apartheid laws. The day is a reminder that it's important to stand up for what is right.

FACT

Major religions in South Africa include Christianity, Hinduism, Judaism, and Islam.

People take part in the Nelson Mandela Day celebration march in 2017.

Reconciliation Day is December 16. It became a holiday after the end of apartheid. The day represents working together for peace and unity.

South African Women's Day celebrates the role of women in shaping history. On August 9, 1956, Helen Joseph organized a march for equal rights for all women. About 20,000 women took part in the march.

Nelson Mandela Day is celebrated on July 18th. South Africans honor Mandela's work to promote equal rights and justice for everyone.

CHAPTER SIX

SPORTS AND RECREATION

Sports are a favorite pastime of South Africans. People gather together to watch sports. Favorite sports in South Africa are soccer, rugby, and cricket.

South Africa won the Rugby World Cup in 1995, 2007, and 2019. After the 1995 win, Nelson Mandela hugged the captain, Francois Pienaar, a white Afrikaner. This represented the future of South Africa by creating an invitation for healing.

THE WORLD CUP

The World Cup is one of the world's largest soccer competitions. South Africa hosted the 2010 World Cup. To prepare for this big event, a new airport and five new stadiums were built. Workers also improved roads. More than 3 million people attended the games.

A national soccer team fan stands near the stadium in Johannesburg in 2021.

KGATI

Kgati is an outdoor game. Three people play it with a jump rope.

1. Choose two people who will swing the rope.
2. The third person will jump the rope in different ways while singing and chanting.
3. The goal is to show creativity and skill while jumping rope and not letting the rope hit your legs.
4. The winner is the person with the best performance.

Tennis is a popular sport. In 1891, the first South African Championships were held. Today, this tournament is called the South African Open. Players from South Africa have become finalists in Grand Slam tournaments.

FACT

Diketo is a traditional game in South Africa. Players throw pebbles or marbles and try to catch them.

South African women's national cricket team member Shabnim Ismail plays during an international match in 2022.

Many South Africans enjoy cricket. The oldest cricket club, Port Elizabeth Cricket Club, formed in 1843. The national cricket team is the Proteas.

A SPECIAL COUNTRY

South Africa is a special country. Visitors can see many landmarks and interesting places. Food, music, and sports provide a connection among people. It is a place rich in history and culture.

GLOSSARY

apartheid (uh-PAR-tayt)
a former policy of racial segregation and discrimination in South Africa

colony (KAH-luh-nee)
an area that has been settled by people from another country; a colony is ruled by another country

culture (KUHL-chuhr)
a people's way of life, ideas, art, customs, and traditions

democratic (de-muh-KRA-tik)
having a kind of government in which citizens vote for their leaders

diversity (duh-VUR-suh-tee)
having different cultural and ethnic backgrounds

ethnic (ETH-nik)
relating to a group of people sharing the same national origins, language, or culture

fossil (FAH-suhl)
the remains or traces of plants and animals that are preserved as rock

Indigenous (in-DIH-jen-us)
a way to describe the first people who lived in a certain area

protest (pro-TEST)
to object to something strongly and publicly

segregation (seg-ruh-GAY-shuhn)
the practice of keeping people of different races apart in schools and other public places

species (SPEE-sheez)
a group of plants or animals that share common characteristics

READ MORE

Juarez, Christine. *Africa: A 4D Book*. North Mankato: Capstone, 2019.

Norry, E. L. *The Extraordinary Life of Nelson Mandela*. Tulsa, OK: Kane Miller, A Division of EDC Publishing, 2020.

Whipple, Annette. *Africa*. North Mankato: Rourke Educational Media, 2019.

INTERNET SITES

Britannica Kids: South Africa
kids.britannica.com/kids/article/South-Africa/345787

Kiddle: South Africa Facts for Kids
kids.kiddle.co/South_Africa

National Geographic Kids: South Africa Facts!
natgeokids.com/uk/discover/geography/countries/facts-about-south-africa/

INDEX

ABOUT THE AUTHOR

Dr. Artika R. Tyner is a passionate educator, award-winning author, a civil rights attorney, a sought-after speaker, and an advocate for justice. She lives in Minneapolis, Minnesota, and is the founder of the Planting People Growing Justice Leadership Institute.

SELECT BOOKS IN THIS SERIES

YOUR PASSPORT TO AUSTRALIA
YOUR PASSPORT TO BRAZIL
YOUR PASSPORT TO EGYPT
YOUR PASSPORT TO ENGLAND

YOUR PASSPORT TO GERMANY
YOUR PASSPORT TO JAPAN
YOUR PASSPORT TO KENYA
YOUR PASSPORT TO MEXICO